PHONICS CONNECTIONS

A Visit to the Library

by Lisa Shulman

Table of Contents

capstone classroom

Let's Go to the Library!

A library is a special place. It has a lot of books on each shelf, but it is not a bookstore. Books in the library are not for sale. Library books are borrowed and brought back at a later date.

People like to use the library. We can use it for free. The library is a good place to read and learn. Let's find out more!

PUBLIC
LIBRARY

Big, Small, or with Wheels

There are different kinds of libraries. Most towns and cities have a public library. Most schools have a library too. Some libraries even move around on wheels!

A public library can be big or small. It has books and other things for people to read and look at. A librarian helps you check out books to take home.

librarian

A school library has books for children and teachers. It has books on many different subjects. You can check out the books to use in class, to help with homework, or just to read for fun.

This library is in a van called a bookmobile. The bookmobile brings books to places that do not have libraries. It may stop near homes or at a shopping mall. Who is the driver? Usually it's the librarian!

The Library of Congress is our national library. It is in Washington, D.C. This library is huge! In fact, it is the biggest library in the world.

Finding Books and More

A public library has thousands of books. It also has newspapers and magazines. It may have games, maps, films, and music too.

Each of these things is kept in its own place. This makes it easy to find what we need. Online catalogs, which are found on computers, can help us find things in a library.

Children's books are kept in the children's room. A children's librarian usually works there. Books for adults are in the main part of the library.

The books on fiction shelves are organized by the author's last name. Librarians place these books on the shelves from A to Z. This alphabetical order can help us find the books we want or need.

Most libraries use special numbers or letters to put nonfiction books in order. Books on the same subject have similar numbers.

Let's Use It!

The library's online catalog helps us find books. It can be fun to use! The librarian can show us how.

We can look up a book's title or the last name of the author. We can also look for a book by its subject. Let's see how this works on the computer.

Let's say that you need a book about pandas. Type the word panda on the computer. The screen will show a list of books about pandas. A book's number helps you find it on the shelf.

You will need a library card to check out books. Most public libraries offer free cards. The librarian can tell you how to get a card.

Show your card when you check out books. Take care of the books you borrow. Remember to return them on time. These rules help make the library a place we can all enjoy!

Index